CONTEMPORARY ISSUES IN HUMAN RESOURCE MANAGEMENT

INTRODUCTION

The human resource management today operates very differently from the human resource management of only a decade ago. Human resource managers face a myriad challenges with today's workforce. There are issues concerning the diverse workforce, legislation affecting the workplace and technology matters that rise to the top of the list of contemporary issues. Business owners need to understand the contemporary issues that human resources managers face, so that they may understand how to utilize this valuable resource to the best advantage.

CONTEMPORARY ISSUES FACED BY HUMAN RESOURCE MANAGERS TODAY

- *Millennials Are on the March*

A generation of employees who were pampered and scheduled by their Baby Boomer parents has taken the workplace by storm.

They bring pluses and minuses to your workplace, but come on, who ever heard of a play date before 1990? So, not only is your workplace trying to absorb these offspring of the Baby Boomer generation.

Millennials and Gen X employees are supervising Boomers and Boomers are mentoring those who wish to learn from the leaving generation.

For the employer, managing millennials is a skill managers need to develop.

The millennial quest for work-life balance and for having a life outside of work is legend.

Employers accommodate these talented young people and develop their strengths and ability to contribute.

- *Employee Training and Development Transformed*

This decade has seen the rise of technology-enabled opportunities for training, employee development, and training meetings and seminars.

Additionally, during this decade, as the technology-enabled delivery options expanded, so did other training and development opportunities and definitions, including increased expectation for learning transfer to the job.

Online learning, earning an online degree or credits, and all forms of web-enabled education and training provide options that employees never had when training occurred in a classroom.

- *Government Intervention in the Employer-Employee Relationship*

A debate exists between people who think the government is already intervening too much by making laws that require employers to provide particular benefits for employees, and those who don't and same in most developing countries.

People who support the government intervention believe that the US government has been negligent in not mandating benefits such as paid sick leave and argument is the same in other countries.

Opponents argue that employer mandated benefits will cost the country jobs and opportunity.

- *The Big Blur*

Online, all the time, and availability via technology, has blurred the line between work and home.

Employees work at home in the evening on collaborative reports and email. They shop at work and take brief breaks by playing online games.

Employees do their banking at work and their work accounting at almost no one goes on vacation without their smart phone, laptop, and kindle-like device.

No Human Resources trend list would be complete without an explicit mention of the impact of technology on all aspects of the field.

Technology has transformed the way in which Human Resources offices manage and communicate employee information and communicate with employees, in general.

- *The Rising Cost of Health Care*

The continually rising cost of health care insurance and health care is affecting what employers can provide in terms of additional benefits for their employees.

- *It's the Economy*

No one can predict how bad the economy could become or how long the downturn will last. So, business leaders don't know whether they are managing from an economic perspective that the economy has been reset forever or a down economy that will recover.

Business leaders are struggling to manage in times they have never before experienced.

- *Employee Recruiting and Networking Online*

This decade has brought about the transformation of employee recruiting and social and media interaction and networking

Employers have seen a transformation in how people find each other for networking and jobs this decade.

Social media networking is the new way to find employees, find jobs, get answers to questions, build a wide-spread, mutually supportive network of contacts, and keep track of colleagues and friends.

Social media and online recruiting bring the employer new challenges such as:

Developing social media and blogging policies, deciding whether to monitor employee time online, and checking candidate backgrounds online, just scratch the surface of new employer challenges.

- *Made to Order Employment Relationships*

Perhaps it's the push from the millennials, and definitely it's the availability of technology that facilitates the customization, but the made to order work relationship has become a dominant force in the past decade

Teleworking or telecommuting, a rare privilege in the 1990s, has taken workplaces by storm.

Teleworking is not the only component of the new made to order work arrangements.

Flexible anything has become the new norm.

Flexible work hours, flexible four day work weeks, flexible time off for appointments, and the most important trend of all

Additionally, trends such as bringing baby or the family pet to the office also fall within this workplace flexibility.

Superficially, all of these components of the made to order Human Resources employment trend offer benefits for employees.

EMERGING ISSUES IN PEOPLE MANAGEMENT

Flexible working the term describes a range of employment options designed to help employees balance work and home life.

Why use the term "flexible"? It is because flexible working relates to working arrangements where there are a variety of options offered to employees in terms of working time, working location and the pattern of working. For example:

- Part-time working
- Term-time working
- Working from home
- Flexitime
- Career breaks
- Job sharing
- Annual hours contracts
- Mobile working
- Shift swapping

Reasons for flexible working options.

- Most importantly, savings on costs. A business can make substantial savings on overheads if it does not have to provide office and other accommodation for so many employees or if staff can work from home rather than commute into work every day.
- As a way of helping with recruitment and staff retention. There is lots of evidence that flexible working results in better job satisfaction and

Contemporary Human Resource Management Issues

higher staff morale.
- To reflect the changing profile of the workforce. There are more women in the labour market and an ageing population – as a result, it is increasingly common for staff to have caring responsibilities outside work.
- To take advantage of developments in technology – it is now simple and cost-effective for employees to be able to access their employers online and other networked systems, and to communicate digitally with colleagues.
- An increasing need for businesses to be able to deliver services to customers on a 24/7 basis. Flexible working makes it easier for businesses to offer extended opening hours, for example
- The "credit crunch" - some organizations, for example firms of lawyers and accountants, have offered part-time working or career breaks as a method of avoiding or minimizing redundancies
- To meet employment legislation – increasingly the law allows certain groups of employees the legal right to request flexible working.

Situations where flexible working is applicable

Joseph Rowntree Foundation found that flexible working practices were most likely to be found in the following situations:

- In large organizations and businesses
- In public sector organizations
- Where the business does not operate in a highly competitive industry
- Where there are recognized unions
- Where there is a well-established HR function
- Where there is high employee involvement in decision-making

- In workforces with larger proportions of women

Where there is a highly educated workforce who has a large amount of discretion in organizing work (e.g. professions, creative industries).

Possible challenges in flexible working approach

Additional administrative work and "red-tape" involved in setting up and running flexible working.

- The potential loss of customers if key employees reduce their working hours.
- Lower employee productivity.
- Inability to substitute for certain skills if certain employees are absent (a common concern of smaller businesses.
- Managers finding it difficult to manage or administer the flexibility.
- A system of flexible working hours gives employees some choice over the actual times they work their contracted hours.
- Such a system can be a good way of recruiting and retaining staff - since it provides an opportunity for employees to work hours consistent with their other commitments (e.g. child care).
- Most flexible working hours schemes have a period during the day when employees must be present. This is known as "core time". A typical core time would be 10 00 a.m. to 4.00 p.m.
- Other than the core time, employees may choose when they start and finish work within flexible bands at the beginning and end of each day.
- However, there is wide scope for variation depending on the core time, the hours the work place is open and the nature of the business.
- Some schemes also have a flexible band during the middle of the day so that employees have some

choice over the time they take their lunch break.
- Contracted hours (the total hours an employee must work according to their employment contract) are achieved by employees working the core time plus hours of their choice during the flexible bands over an agreed period.
- This period is known as the accounting period and is typically four weeks long.
- Some schemes allow for an excess or deficit (within set limits) to be carried over to the next accounting period
- Hours are credited for absences such as sickness or holidays.

How to introduce a flexible working hours scheme

The introduction of a flexible working hours scheme requires care and needs to be carefully planned by all those likely to be affected.

Experience suggests that a joint "working party" comprising representatives of management and employees is usually the best approach and any recognised trade union should be fully involved.

Whether the scheme is to be voluntary or compulsory

What type of recording system should be used (e.g. manual, clocking or computerized).

How flexibility should be built into the bands

How sickness, absence and late attendance should be treated

Arrangements for managing and monitoring the scheme (e.g. monitoring the effect on production or customer service levels)

Advantages of flexible working hours

- Employees have greater freedom
- Can make traveling easier (e.g. avoiding commuting during the normal rush-hour)
- Improved morale and reducing absence and lateness
- Reduction in overtime and less lost time since long lunch breaks or late arrivals are not recorded as time worked

Disadvantages of flexible working hours

- Costs involved in administering the scheme
- If the premises are open longer, there may be increased costs for lighting and heating
- Employees will not be in work at certain times and therefore it may not be suitable for organizations where continuous cover is necessary.

EMPLOYEE PARTICIPATION

Employee participation is the process whereby employees are involved in decision making processes, rather than simply acting on orders.

Employee participation is part of a process of empowerment in the workplace.
Empowerment involves decentralizing power within the organisation to individual decision makers further down the line.

Team working is a key part of the empowerment process

Team members are encouraged to make decisions for themselves in line with guidelines and frameworks established in self managing teams.

Employee participation is in part a response to the quality movement within organisations.

Employee participation is also part of the move towards human resource development in modern organisations.

Employees are trusted to make decisions for themselves and the organisation

Employee participation is also referred to as employee involvement.

Employee participation methods

- Project teams or quality circles in which employees work on projects or tasks with considerable responsibility being delegated to the team.
- Suggestion schemes - where employees are given channels whereby they can suggest new ideas to managers

within the organization. Often they will receive rewards for making appropriate suggestions.
- Consultation exercises and meetings whereby employees are encouraged to share ideas.
- Delegation of responsibility within the organization. In modern organizations ground level employees have to be given considerable responsibility because they are dealing with customers on a day-to-day basis. Such employees need to be trusted to make decisions for themselves.
- Multi-channel decision making processes. In such situations decisions are not only made in a downward direction, they also result from communications upwards, sideways, and in many other directions within the organization.

Benefits of employee participation

- Employees make better
- Employees make better decisions using their expert knowledge of the process.
- Employees are more likely to implement and support decisions they had a part in making.
- Employees are better able to spot and pinpoint areas of for improvement.
- Employees are better able to take immediate corrective actions.
- Employee involvement reduces labor/management friction by encouraging more effective communication and cooperation.
- Employee involvement increases morale by creating feeling of belonging to the organization.
- Employees are better able to accept change because they control the work environment.
- Employees have an increased commitment to unit goals because they are involved.
- Employee involvement and empowerment trans-

lates directly into increased productivity
- Employee empowerment helps to cultivate innovation

PSYCHOLOGICAL CONTRACT

As commercial organizations grew in size and complexity, there is a tendency to standardize rather than individualize the treatment of labor unions have lost some of their significance, leaving employees in more direct control unlike before where they were engaged in collective bargaining as a way of protecting workers' terms and condition of employment.

Societies have developed expectations of a better work-life balance, reinforced by legislation, and employers have found it in their own best interests to develop practices that respect equal opportunities and employment rights through professionalized human resource services.

Reasons for change

- The workforce has become more feminized;
- The workforce is better educated, less deferential to authority and less likely to remain loyal;
- The workforce is required to be more flexible to meet new challenges quickly and effectively, but this need to change can be a source of insecurity;
- The use of temporary workers as well as outsourcing of projects and whole business functions also changes workers' expectations as to what they want to get out of their psychological contracts (e.g., transferable skills now vs. life-time employment before); and
- Automation has both empowered a greater percentage of the workforce and allowed the emergence of teleworking which fragments the old social orders of a single location workplace and gen-

erates greater freedom and flexibility in an ever increasing global workforce.

The formation of a psychological contract

During the recruitment process, the employer and interviewee will discuss what they each can offer in the prospective relationship

If agreement is reached, most employers will impose a standard form contract, leaving the detail of the employee's duties to be clarified "on the job".

But some of the initial statements, no matter how informal and imprecise, may later be remembered as promises and give rise to expectations.

Better organized employers are careful to document offers to reduce the risk of raising false expectations followed by disappointment.

In the Common Law jurisdictions, the law implies duties requiring the employees to be loyal and trustworthy.

These are imprecise in their definition and uncertain in much of their operation

But, in psychological terms, issues as to whether promises and expectations have been kept and met, and whether the resulting arrangements are fair, are fundamental to the trust between the employee and the employer.

The first year of employment is critical as actual performance by the employee can be measured against claims and promises made during the interview, and the management has begun to establish a track record in its relationship with the employee at supervisor and manager level.

Feldhiem (1999) reflects these two strands by dividing the psychological contract into:

- Transactional: this is the economic or monetary

base with clear expectations that the organization will fairly compensate the performance delivered and punish inadequate or inappropriate acts; and
- Relational: this is a socio-emotional base that underlies expectations of shared ideals and values, and respect and support in the interpersonal relationships.

Breach of the psychological contract

Psychological contract breach may occur if employees perceive that their firm, or its agents, have failed to deliver on what they perceive was promised, or vice versa.

Employees or employers who perceive a breach are likely to respond negatively

Responses may occur in the form of reduced loyalty, commitment, and organizational citizenship behaviors.

Perceptions that once psychological contract has been breached may arise shortly after the employee joins the company or even after years of satisfactory service.

The impact may be localized and contained, but if morale is more generally affected, the performance of the organization may be diminished

Further, if the activities of the organization are perceived as being unjust or immoral, e.g. aggressive downsizing or outsourcing causing significant unemployment, its public reputation and brand image may also be damaged.

TELEWORKING

Teleworking is a method of workforce planning that allows employees to spend all or part of their working week at a location remote from employers' workplaces.

Home working is a form of teleworking but there are several different categories:

- Traditional mobile workers like sales representatives and delivery drivers. They receive instructions and information via telephones, computers or fax machines at home or in their vehicles;
- Managerial and professional staff who spend working days away from their office base and also communicate via telephones, computers or fax machines from their home car or other remote location;
- Specialists or office support staff who carry out a range of duties from home or other remote locations and communicate via telephones fax machines and computers;
- Other workers who operate from local centres with computer and telecommunications facilities sometimes known as 'telecottages'

Advantages of Teleworking

- Teleworking can reduce costs by providing savings on office space and other facilities.
- It can improve productivity as people are not interrupted by the day to day distractions of office life and politics.

- Employees have more freedom over where they live, how they organize their work and when they carry it out.
- Employers who help people with disabilities or caring responsibilities to work at home can benefit from the additional skills and expertise of workers who may not be available to attend the workplace.
- Teleworking also reduces or eliminates time spent on traveling and lowers absence and turnover rates.

Disadvantages of Teleworking

- Remote working is not suitable for all types of job
- Providing suitable technology can be expensive
- Some employees may feel socially isolated; successful teleworkers tend to be self motivated, self-disciplined, competent and able to work with little supervision
- Despite improvements in communications technology, managers may find it difficult to communicate with and manage remote workers
- Career development and training may suffer
- Health and safety issues arise - are employees' homes or other available premises suitable for teleworking?

CHANGE MANAGEMENT

Components of change management include:

- Change management process
- Readiness assessments
- Communication and communication planning
- Coaching and manager training for change management
- Training and employee training development
- Sponsor activities and sponsor roadmaps
- Resistance management
- Data collection, feedback analysis and corrective action
- Celebrating and recognizing success

Change management process

The change management process is the sequence of steps or activities that a change management team or project leader would follow to apply change management to a project or change.

Change management processes contain the following three phases:

- Phase 1 - Preparing for change (Preparation, assessment and strategy development)
- Phase 2 - Managing change (Detailed planning and change management implementation)
- Phase 3 - Reinforcing change (Data gathering, corrective action and recognition)

READINESS ASSESSMENTS

Assessments are tools used by a change management team or project leader to assess the organization's readiness to change

Assessments can include organizational assessments, culture and history assessments, employee assessments, sponsor assessments and change assessments

Aspects that can be assess on readiness

Assess the scope of the change, including: How big is this change? How many people are affected? Is it a gradual or radical change?

Assess the readiness of the organization impacted by the change, including: What is the value- system and background of the impacted groups? How much change is already going on? What type of resistance can be expected?

Assess the strengths of your change management team.

Assess the change sponsors and take the first steps to enable them to effectively lead the change process.

Communication and communication planning

Many managers assume that if they communicate clearly with their employees, their job is done. However, there are many reasons why employees may not hear or understand what their managers are saying the first time around

Effective communicators carefully consider three components: the audience, what is said and when it is said.

The first step in managing change is building awareness around the need for change and creating a desire among employees.

Initial communications are typically designed to create awareness around the business reasons for change and the risk of not changing.

At each step in the process, communications should be designed to share the right messages at the right time.

Communication planning, therefore, begins with a careful analysis of the audiences, key messages and the timing for those messages.

The change management team or project leaders must design a communication plan that addresses the needs of frontline employees, supervisors and executives.

Coaching and manager training for change management

Supervisors will play a key role in managing change. , the direct supervisor has more influence over an employee's motivation to change than any other person at work.

- supervisors as a group can be the most difficult to convince of the need for change and can be a source of resistance

- It is vital for the change management team and executive sponsors to gain the support of supervisors and to build change leadership.

TRAINING AND TRAINING DEVELOPMENT

Training is the cornerstone for building knowledge about the change and the required skills.

Project team members will develop training requirements based on the skills, knowledge and behaviors necessary to implement the change

These training requirements will be the starting point for the training group or the project team to develop training programs.

Sponsor activities and sponsor roadmaps

Business leaders and executives play a critical sponsor role in change management.

Change management team must develop a plan for sponsor activities and help key business leaders carry out these plans

Sponsorship should be viewed as the most important success factor.

Sponsorship involves active and visible participation by senior business leaders throughout the process

A change agent's or project leader's role includes helping senior executives do the right things to sponsor the project

RESISTANCE MANAGEMENT

Resistance from employees and managers is normal

The change management team needs to identify, understand and manage resistance throughout the organization

Resistance management is the processes and tools used by managers and executives with the support of the project team to manage employee resistance.

Data collection, feedback analysis and corrective action

Employee involvement is a necessary and integral part of managing change

Managing change is not a one way street. Feedback from employees is a key element of the change management process.

Analysis and corrective action based on this feedback provides a robust cycle for implementing change.

Celebrating and recognizing success

Early successes and long-term wins must be recognized and celebrated

Individual and group recognition is also a necessary component of change management in order to cement and reinforce the change in the organization.

The final step in the change management process is the after-action review

It is at this point that you can stand back from the entire program, evaluate successes and failures, and identify process changes for the next project.

This is part of the ongoing, continuous improvement of change management for your organization and ultimately leads to change competency.

Specific Reasons for resistance

- Economic reasons – change may threaten the economic well – being of employees in the company, this creates a lot of economic uncertainty for the individuals concerned and naturally people do not like uncertainties about their future.
- Social reasons – change can threaten to break the informal structures in an organization and as such any threat to established informal groups tends to be resisted by the members.
- Status reasons – change in the organization may reduce the perceived status of some individuals in the organization therefore they resist such changes.
- Security reasons – people always crave for economic physical and psychological security. Any changes that create uncertainly over such security will be resisted.
- Maintenance of status quo – change is frequently resisted because it is easier for people to maintain the status quo i.e. people to maintain the status quo.

HUMAN RESOURCE STRATEGIC CHANGE

A transformational power in HRM and transformation, or change, is an inevitable consequence of many human resource strategies

Bertsch and Williams identified two main types of change:

- Turnaround change - financially driven, often to ensure corporate survival by cutting unprofitable products and services. It involves the redesign of organizational structures, disposal of non-core activities and large-scale redundancies.
- Behavioural transformations – changing behaviour patterns throughout the company. Hierarchical control is inadequate because different power centers are likely to conflict and differences between business units make behavioural consistency a difficult objective to achieve.

CHANGE MANAGEMENT

- Communication and interpersonal57 skills: well developed negotiating and listening skills and the ability to build relationships.
- Organisational ability and time management skills.
- Excellent attention to detail, as you may need to conduct or interpret salary surveys and analyse data.
- Excellent professional responsibility and ethics, as the work may involve reference checking, dealing with employment legislation and maintaining confidential records.
- Sound commercial awareness, in order to understand the wider business context that the firm is operating in.
- Strong numerical ability, for roles that focus on the more financial or numerical aspects of HR, such as compensation, benefits and pensions.

How Human Resource Can Deliver Change Management Results

Human Resource can deliver these impressive results through a powerful combination of new paradigms, a principle-based approach to change which simultaneously promotes stability and the management of the organization The approach will enable Human Resource to:

- Accelerate the pace of sustainable change,
- Increase commitment to needed changes, and

- Develop greater capacity for future change in the organization.

SKILL BUILDING

Skill building is enhancement of personnel skills through training and development programmes established in an organization

To succeed in today's workplace involves more than just having a number of advanced qualifications. As the economy is still somewhat stagnant, those individuals with the broadest career skills are likely to take up the most interesting and well paid positions.

Advancement should always be at the forefront of a driven person's mind when they consider the current condition and future of their career.

In order for advancement to truly and effectively be acquired, career leadership must be a top priority.

Almost all businesses require personnel to make it in the market. Whether you are in the production or services sector, staff members play a very significant role in ensuring the success or failure of your business

Employee development is necessary if organization is to expect business to prosper

Employees need to be multi skilled and rich skilled in order to better their career development and at the sometime improve organization performance. This can be done through' training and re-training to equip with the necessary skills

PERFORMANCE REWARDS

To ensure the reward system is effective and motivates the desired behaviors, it is essential to consider carefully the rewards and strategies utilized and ensure the rewards are linked to or based on performance.

To be effective, any performance measurement system must be tied to compensation or some sort of reward.

Rewarding performance should be an ongoing managerial activity, not just an annual pay-linked ritual.

Strategies for rewarding employees' performance and contributions include both non-financial and financial mechanisms. Some of the primary ones are discussed below.

- Praise/recognition from supervisors - Praise and recognition from supervisors is consistently found to be among the most important motivators.
- Challenging work assignments - Challenging/new work assignments are another mechanism available to supervisors to reward good performance. Such assignments can provide employees opportunities to develop new skills, expand their knowledge, and/or increase their visibility within the organization.
- Professional growth and development opportunities- Supervisors may provide employees opportunities to participate in educational programs or other activities that will expand their skills/knowledge
- Employees benefit by developing new skills, and

the institution benefits from the additional expertise individuals bring to the job.
- Progression through the salary range - Employees may receive salary increases to recognize the attainment of new and/or the enhancement of existing skills/competencies or for assuming increased responsibilities within the scope of the current position.
- Merit increases - UT-Houston policy allows supervisors to give employees an annual merit increase to recognize consistently meritorious performance or successful completion of a project that had a significant impact on a department or the university.
- Lump Sum Merit- A lump sum merit is a one-time award, not added to base pay, that can be awarded to an individual for meritorious job performance. Meritorious job performance is defined as either consistently high level of job performance over a sustained period of time;
- Promotions and lateral moves - Promotions and lateral moves may be long term rewards that recognize employees' professional growth, expertise, and capacity to contribute to the institution in new roles.
- Administrative salary supplements - Employees who assume new/additional responsibilities on an interim basis may receive administrative salary supplements that are paid in addition to the base salary. The supplement is discontinued when the employee is no longer responsible for the additional responsibilities.
- Informal rewards - When warranted, supervisors may choose to give employees informal rewards for specific accomplishments/contributions.

Supervisors can be creative in identifying informal rewards that will be appreciated by the particular individual being recognized, but, in selecting and purchasing rewards, supervisors must be sensitive to the institution's responsibility to be good stewards of public funds.

WORK-LIFE

A specific set of organizational practices, policies, programs, plus a philosophy, which actively supports efforts to help employees achieve success at both work and

Work-life programs encompass compensation, benefits and other HR programs, and together they address the key intersections of the worker, his or her family, the community and the workplace.

Seven categories of support for work-life effectiveness

Creating Workplace Flexibility A variety of flexible work options that enable greater control over when, where and how work gets done.

- The Creative Use of Paid and Unpaid Time off Personal time away from work to spend with family, friends and self. Governmental regulations vary dramatically by country in terms of how much time an employee can or must take, and whether for not that time is paid by the employer.
- Supporting Health and Wellness Health and wellness initiatives focus on reducing absenteeism and improving productivity by supporting healthy lifestyle choices for employees and their families.
- Community Involvement The way organizations get involved with the external and internal community through monetary donations, volunteer programs and partnerships.
- Caring for Dependents There are many issues related to caregiving for dependents of all ages. Most organiza-

tions offer some type of support for parenting and elder care.
- Financial Support In the area of financial support, work-life is primarily concerned with gaining approval for, and helping implement, voluntary financial benefits as well as providing resources and referrals that assist employees with managing their financial responsibilities.
- Culture Change Initiatives Organizational culture consists of the collective attitudes and behaviors of individuals within the organization. Changing cultures is challenging because it involves changing these attitudes and behaviors through altering the beliefs and values that are behind them.

HUMAN RESOURCE AS INTERNAL CONSULTANT

Categories:

- Process consultant- true collaboration with the client, wherein owns both problems and answers and the consultant's role is a helper
- Expert consultant- where the consultant's currency is defined and solution offered by the consultant
- Pair- of hands consultant- where the client scopes the problem and the solution and the consultant skills are used to solve it.

Definition of an internal consultant?

Typically the internal consultant is drawn from one of the terms of professional service providers such as HR, IT or Finance.

Supporting internal customers with specific problems

Working alongside their colleagues- their clients analyzing problems diagnosing issues and proposing

It deals with process areas such as team building, objective setting, quality management, and customer service.

May be assigned service delivery contracts in such fields as recruitment and training, performance appraisals, occupational health and safety

TALENT MANAGEMENT

Talent management is a term that emerged in the 1990s to incorporate developments in Human Resources Management which placed more of an emphasis on the management of human resources or talent.

Talent management is part of the Evolution of Talent Measurement Technologies

The issue with many companies today is that their organizations put tremendous effort into attracting employees to their company, but spend little time into retaining and developing talent

Talent management system must be worked into the business strategy and implemented in daily processes throughout the company as a whole.

The business strategy must include responsibilities for line managers to develop the skills of their immediate subordinates.

Divisions within the company should be openly sharing information with other departments in order for employees to gain knowledge of the overall organizational objectives.

Companies that focus on developing their talent integrate plans and processes to track and manage their employee talent,

Why Talent Management?

Workforce cost is the largest category of spend for most organizations

Automation and analysis of your recruiting and hiring processes provides the immediate workforce visibility and insights you need to significantly improve your bottom line.

Performance management provides the ongoing processes and practices to maintain a stellar workforce.

Today, many organizations are struggling with silos of HR processes and technologies

The future of talent management is embodied in solutions designed from the ground up to provide business-centric functionality on a unified talent management platform.

Ways of managing talent

- Sourcing, attracting, recruiting and on boarding qualified candidates with competitive backgrounds
- Managing and defining competitive salaries
- Training and development opportunities
- Performance management processes
- Retention programs
- Promotion and transitioning
- The talent management strategy may be supported by technology such as HRIS (HR Information Systems) or HRMS (HR Management Systems)

Companies that engage in talent management (Human Capital Management) are strategic and deliberate in how they source, attract, select, train, develop, retain, promote, and move employees through the organization

The major aspects of talent management practiced within an organization must consistently include:

- Performance management
- Leadership development
- Workforce planning/identifying talent gaps
- Recruiting

Talent supply chain management

Talent Supply Chain Management is a proactive management approach to securing and optimizing talent supply and services through all input channels (supplier network) to meet the human capital (workforce) needs of companies, enabling them to better produce, distribute and deliver their goods and services and meet their strategic objectives.

LEADERSHIP DEVELOPMENT

Leadership development refers to any activity that enhances the quality of leadership within an individual or organization.

Developing Individual Leaders

Traditionally, leadership development has focused on developing the leadership abilities and attitudes of individuals.

The success of leadership development efforts has been linked to three variables:

- Individual learner characteristics
- The quality and nature of the leadership development program
- Genuine support for behavioural change from the leader's supervisor

Development is also more likely to occur when the design of the development program:

Integrates a range of developmental experiences over a set period of time (e.g. 6-12 months). These experiences may include 360 degree feedback, experiential classroom style programs, business school style coursework, executive coaching, mentoring etc.

Involve goal setting, following an assessment of key developmental needs and then evaluate the achievement of goals after a given time period.

Personal characteristics that associated with successful leadership development include leader motivation to learn, a high achievement drive and personality traits such as openness to experience, an internal focus of control, and self-monitoring.

Both forms of development may mutually influence each other, as exemplified in the concept of "Deep Change" in Robert E. Quinn 1996

Leadership development can build on the development of individuals (including followers) to become leaders. In addition, it also needs to focus on the interpersonal linkages between the individuals in the team.

Key concepts in leadership development

Among key concepts in leadership development one may find:

- Experiential learning: positioning the individual in the focus of the learning process, going through the four stages of experiential learning as formulated by David A. Kolb:
    i. Concrete experience
    ii. Observation and reflection
    iii. Forming abstract concept
    iv. testing in new situations.
- Self-efficacy: The right training and coaching should bring about 'Self efficacy' in the trainee, as Albert Bandura formulated: A person's belief about his capabilities to produce effects
- Visioning: Developing the ability to formulate a clear image of the aspired future of an organization unit.

Leadership development program

A good personal leadership development program should enable you to develop a plan that helps you gain essential leadership skills required for roles across a wide spectrum.

These characteristics include:

- Taking responsibility
- Gaining focus

- Developing life purpose
- Starting action immediately
- Developing effective and achievable goals and dreams

Developing Leadership at a Collective Level

More recently, organizations have come to understand that leadership can also be developed by strengthening the connection between, and alignment of, the efforts of individual leaders and the systems through which they influence organizational operations.

This has led to a differentiation between leader development and leadership development

Leader development focuses on the development of the leader, such as the personal attributes desired in a leader, desired ways of behaving, ways of thinking or feeling.

Leadership development focuses on the development of leadership as a process.

This will include the interpersonal relationships, social influence process, and the team dynamics between the leader and his/her team, the contextual factors surrounding the team such as the perception of the organizational climate and the social network linkages between the team and other groups in the organization.

Leadership development can build on the development of individuals (including followers) to become leaders.

OUTSOURCING

Outsourcing is the act of one company contracting with another company to provide services that might otherwise be performed by in-house employees.

Often the tasks that are outsourced could be performed by the company itself, but in many cases there are financial advantages that come from outsourcing.

Reasons to Outsource

- There are many reasons that companies outsource various jobs, but the most prominent advantage seems to be the fact that it often saves money
- Companies that provide outsourcing services are able to do the work for considerably less money
- Outsourcing also allows companies to focus on other business issues while having the details taken care of by outside experts.
- The specialized company that handles the outsourced work is often streamlined, and often has world-class capabilities and access to new technology
- Depending on location, it may also be more affordable to outsource to companies located in different countries.

The advantages of outsourcing

- Focus on core activities

In rapid growth periods, the back-office operations of a company will expand also. This expansion may start to consume resources (human and financial) at the expense of the core activities that have made your company successful

- Cost and efficiency savings

Back-office functions that are complicated in nature, but the size of your company is preventing you from performing it at a consistent and reasonable cost, is another advantage of outsourcing.

- Reduced overhead

Overhead costs of performing a particular back-office function are extremely high. Consider outsourcing those functions which can be moved easily.

- Operational control

Operations whose costs are running out of control must be considered for outsourcing.

- Staffing flexibility

Outsourcing will allow operations that have seasonal or cyclical demands to bring in additional resources when you need them and release them when you're done.

- Continuity & risk management

Periods of high employee turnover will add uncertainty and inconsistency to the operations. Outsourcing will provided a level of continuity to the company while reducing the risk that a substandard level of operation would bring to the company.

- Develop internal staff

A large project needs to be undertaken that requires skills that your staff does not possess. On-site outsourcing of the project will bring people with the skills you need into your company. Your people can work alongside of them to acquire the new skill set.

Disadvantages of Outsourcing

- Risk of exposing confidential data: When an organization outsources HR, Payroll and Recruitment services, it

involves a risk if exposing confidential company information to a third-party.
- Synchronizing the deliverables: In case you do not choose a right partner for outsourcing, some of the common problem areas include stretched delivery time frames, sub-standard quality output and inappropriate categorization of responsibilities
- Hidden costs: Although outsourcing most of the times is costeffective at times the hidden costs involved in signing a contract while signing a contract across international boundaries may pose a serious threat.
- Lack of customer focus: An outsourced vendor may be catering to the expertise-needs of multiple organizations at a time

Benefits of Outsourcing

- Lower costs

Lower costs are perhaps the prime benefit of offshore outsourcing.

- Skilled Expertise

Finding skilled resources is one of the biggest challenges faced by companies today, not to mention the investment required to train employees and the attendant infrastructure required, which can rapidly drain funds.

- Time zone difference

Because of the time zone difference between Asian countries and the West, you can get your work done while your business closes down in the evening.

- Focus on core competencies

As a company grows, administrative functions also grow. Managing back-office operations and administrative functions takes the time and energy out of any organization

- Distribution of risk

When certain functions are outsourced, companies also distribute or do away with the risks associated with running that particular function.

- Improving customer service

Customer service is paramount to any organization. Through outsourcing you can service your customers faster, provide better quality and decrease turnaround time.

- Better people management

Since outsourcing takes care of the skills necessary to run a particular business process, your business is much more flexible in investing in key resources.

WORKPLACE DIVERSITY

Diversity in this context covers gender, age, language, ethnicity, cultural background, sexual orientation, religious belief and family responsibilities.

Diversity also refers to the other ways in which people are different, such as educational level, life experience, work experience, socioeconomic background, personality and marital status

Workplace diversity involves recognizing the value of individual differences and managing them in the workplace.

Managing diversity successfully means creating an environment that values and utilizes the contributions of people with different backgrounds, experiences and perspectives.

Organizations need to develop people management strategies that accommodate differences in the background, perspectives and family responsibilities of their employees

The concept of workplace diversity includes the principle of equal employment opportunity (EEO).

How does workplace diversity fit into the wider organization?

Workplace diversity principles should be integrated with and underpin all aspects of human resource management, such as planning, selection and recruitment, performance appraisal, training and development, occupational health and safety and workplace relations should incorporate flexible working conditions to allow employees to balance their work and other responsibilities.

Workplace diversity strategies help to build the organisation's relationship with the community, enhance the contribution of its employees and improve the quality of its programs, products and services.

Establishing effective workplace diversity programs

Establishing an effective workplace diversity program could involve:

- Considering what the program will achieve;
- Deciding how the program will be developed and implemented;
- Drawing links to organizational objectives;
- Undertaking consultation; and
- Assessing the resources required.

Strategies

- Specify the need for skills to work effectively in a diverse environment in the job, for example: "demonstrated ability to work effectively in a diverse work environment."
- Make sure that good faith efforts are made to recruit a diverse applicant pool, particularly underutilized minorities and women.
- Focus on the job requirements in the interview, and assess experience but also consider
- Transferable skills and demonstrated competencies, such as analytical, organizational, communication, co-ordination. Prior experience has not necessarily mean effectiveness or success on the job.
- Use a panel interview format. Ensure that the committee is diverse, unit affiliation, job classification, length of service, variety of life experiences, etc. to represent different to represent different perspectives and to eliminate bias from the selection process.
- Ensure that appropriate accommodations are made for disabled applicants.
- Know your own biases. What stereotypes do you have

of people from different groups and how well they may perform on the job? What communication styles do you prefer? Sometimes what we consider to be appropriate or desirable qualities in a candidate may reflect more about our personal preferences than about the skills needed to perform the job.

Cultivating an atmosphere of Cultural Diversity among employees

Cultural diversity in the workplace promotes an equal opportunity atmosphere and allows people from all heritages and ethnicities to reach their full career potential.

Under the Federal Equal Employment Opportunity laws in the United States, it is illegal to discriminate against employees or potential employees on the basis of race, culture, ethnicity, gender, disability, religion, political beliefs, or marital status. The same to cultural discrimination in the workplace usually comes about as a result of a lack of understanding of an individual's beliefs and culture.

The application of ethnic stereotypes to an individual based on their actual or perceived race, culture, and beliefs is also responsible for much of the intentional and unintentional, or unconscious social discrimination that occurs in the workplace.

Ways of managing diversity

- By expanding employee recruiting efforts:

Employers who expand their recruiting efforts beyond their usual, established channels will find that they will naturally attract a diverse group of applicants

- Through accommodations and policy revisions:

From physical building modifications to accommodations such as providing sign language interpretation and large print

- By emphasizing similarities:

Instead of focusing on differences, concentrating on the similarities between various groups of people is an effective way to promote understanding of another's perspective.

Cultural awareness training designed to educate both employees and employers about the best ways to interact with and relate to individuals from different backgrounds can go a long way towards eliminating biases and misconceptions.

Employers can also take the time to research the social and business practices associated with the cultural background of their employees

Cultural diversity in the workplace should be both the goal and the responsibility of both employers and employees.

The benefits of diversity

- Increased innovation a diverse workforce with a range of different backgrounds and perspectives gives organizations a broader range of ideas and insights to draw on in decision making and policy development..
- Improved service to clients A workplace that reflects the community will understand its clients better, which will lead to improved service. A diverse workplace will have good communication with its clients based on a deep understanding of the needs of the community.
- Competitive management practices organizations that value and capitalize on employee diversity have productive and fulfilling workplaces which help them attract and retain employees.
- Modelling what we promote, it helps in promoting principles of equity and productive diversity in the employment practices.

WORKPLACE BULLYING

Workplace bullying, like childhood bullying, is the tendency of individuals or groups to use persistent aggressive or unreasonable behavior against a co-worker or subordinate.

Workplace bullying can include such tactics as verbal, nonverbal, psychological, physical abuse and humiliation.

This type of aggression is particularly difficult because, unlike the typical forms of school bullying, workplace bullies often operate within the established rules and policies of their organization and their society

Bullying in the workplace is in the majority of cases reported as having been perpetrated by management and takes a wide variety of forms.

Definition

While there is no single formal definition of workplace bullying, several researchers have endeavored to define it

According to Tracy, Lutgen-Sandvik, and Alberts, researchers associated with the Project for Wellness and Work-Life, workplace bullying is most often "a combination of tactics in which numerous types of hostile communication and behaviour are used"

Pamela Lutgen-Sandvik expands this definition, stating that workplace bullying is "persistent verbal and nonverbal aggression at work, that includes personal attacks, social ostracism, and a multitude of other painful messages and hostile interactions

Typology of bullying behaviours

- Threat to professional status - including belittling opinions, public professional humiliation, accusations regarding lack of effort, intimidating use of discipline or competence procedures
- Threat to personal standing - including undermining personal integrity, destructive innuendo and sarcasm, making inappropriate jokes about target, persistent teasing, name calling, insults, intimidation
- Isolation - including preventing access to opportunities, physical or social isolation, withholding necessary information, keeping the target out of the loop, ignoring or excluding
- Overwork - including undue pressure, impossible deadlines, unnecessary disruptions.
- Destabilization - including failure to acknowledge good work, allocation of meaningless tasks, removal of responsibility, repeated reminders of blunders, setting target up to fail, shifting goal posts without telling the target.

Most common 25 tactics used by workplace bullies:

- Falsely accused someone of "errors" not actually made (71 percent).
- Stared, glared, was nonverbally intimidating and was clearly showing hostility (68 percent).
- Discounted the person's thoughts or feelings ("oh, that's silly") in meetings (64 percent).
- Used the "silent treatment" to "ice out" and separate from others (64 percent).
- Exhibited presumably uncontrollable mood swings in front of the group (61 percent).
- Made up own rules on the fly that even she/he did not follow (61 percent).

Contemporary Human Resource Management Issues

- Abused the evaluation process by lying about the person's performance (46 percent).
- Disregarded satisfactory or exemplary quality of completed work despite evidence (discrediting) (58 percent).
- Harshly and constantly criticized having a different standard for the target (57 percent).
- Started, or failed to stop, destructive rumors or gossip about the person (56 percent).
- Encouraged people to turn against the person being tormented (55 percent).
- Singled out and isolated one person from other coworkers, either socially or physically (54 percent).
- Publicly displayed gross, undignified, but not illegal, behavior (53 percent).
- Yelled, screamed, threw tantrums in front of others to humiliate a person (53 percent).
- Stole credit for work done by others (plagiarism) (47 percent).
- Abused the evaluation process by lying about the person's performance (46 percent).
- Declared target "insubordinate" for failing to follow arbitrary commands (46 percent).
- Used confidential information about a person to humiliate privately or publicly (45 percent).
- Retaliated against the person after a complaint was filed (45 percent).
- Made verbal put-downs/insults based on gender, race, accent, age or language, disability (44 percent).
- Assigned undesirable work as punishment (44 percent).
- Created unrealistic demands (workload, deadlines, duties) for person singled out (44 percent).
- Launched a baseless campaign to oust the person; effort not stopped by the employer (43 percent).
- Encouraged the person to quit or transfer rather than to face more mistreatment (43 percent).

- Sabotaged the person's contribution to a team goal and reward (41 percent).
- Ensured failure of person's project by not performing required tasks, such as sign-offs, taking calls, working with collaborators (40 percent)

According to Bassman, common abusive workplace behaviours:

- Disrespecting and devaluing the individual, often through disrespectful and devaluing language or verbal abuse
- Overwork and devaluation of personal life (particularly salaried workers who are not compensated)
- Harassment through micromanagement of tasks and time
- Overevaluation and manipulating information (for example concentration on negative characteristics and failures, setting up subordinate for failure).
- Managing by threat and intimidation
- Stealing credit and taking unfair advantage
- Preventing access to opportunities
- Downgrading an employee's capabilities to justify downsizing
- Impulsive destructive behaviour

Why do people bully?

a) To avoid facing up to their inadequacy and doing something about it;
b) To avoid accepting responsibility for their behaviour and the effect it has on others, and,
c) To reduce their fear of being seen for what they are, namely a weak, inadequate and often incompetent individuals, and,
d) To divert attention away from their inadequacy - in an insecure or badly-managed workplace, this is how inadequate, incompetent and aggressive employees keep their jobs.

A bully is a person who:

- Has never learnt to accept responsibility for their behavior
- Wants to enjoy the benefits of living in the adult world, but who is unable and unwilling to accept the responsibilities that are a prerequisite for being part of the adult world.
- Abdicates and denies responsibility for their behaviour and its consequences (abdication and denial are common features of bullying)
- Is unable and unwilling to recognize the effect of their behaviour on others
- Does not want to know of any other way of behaving
- Is unwilling to recognize that there could be better ways of behaving.

How to spot a bully in your workplace

- Staff turnover
- Sickness absence
- Stress breakdowns
- Deaths in service
- Ill-health retirements
- Early retirements
- Uses of disciplinary procedures
- Grievances initiated
- Suspensions
- Dismissals
- Uses of private security firms to snoop on employees
- Litigation including employment tribunals or legal action against employees

Types of bullying

- Pressure bullying or unwitting bullying is where the stress of the moment causes behaviour to deteriorate; the person becomes short-tempered, irritable and may shout or swear at others
- Organizational bullying is a combination of pressure

bullying and corporate bullying, and occurs when an organization struggles to adapt to changing markets, reduced income, cuts in budgets, imposed expectations, and other external pressures.
- Corporate bullying is where the employer abuses employees with impunity knowing that the law is weak and jobs are scarce,
- Institutional bullying is similar to corporate bullying and arises when bullying becomes entrenched and accepted as part of the culture. People are moved, long-existing contracts are replaced with new short-term contracts on less favourable terms with the accompanying threat of "agree to this or else"
- Client bullying is where employees are bullied by those they serve, eg teachers are bullied (and often assaulted) by pupils and their parents, nurses are bullied by patients and their relatives, social workers are bullied by their clients, and shop/bank/building society staff are bullied by customers.
- Serial bullying is where the source of all dysfunction can be traced to one individual, who picks on one employee after another and destroys them.
- Secondary bullying is mostly unwitting bullying which people start exhibiting when there's a serial bully in the department. The pressure of trying to deal with a dysfunctional, divisive and aggressive serial bully causes everyone's behaviour to decline.
- Pair bullying is a serial bully with a colleague. Often one does the talking whilst the other watches and listens. Usually it's the quiet one you need to watch
- Gang bullying is a serial bully with colleagues. Gangs can occur anywhere, but flourish in corporate bullying climates.

- Regulation bullying is where a serial bully forces their target to comply with rules, regulations, procedures or laws regardless of their appropriateness, applicability or necessity.
- Residual bullying is the bullying of all kinds that continues after the serial bully has left. Like recruits like and like promotes like, therefore the serial bully bequeaths a dysfunctional environment to those who are left. This can last for years.
- Cyber bullying is the misuse of email systems or Internet forums etc for sending aggressive flame mails. Serial bullies have few communication skills (and often none), thus the impersonal nature of email makes it an ideal tool for causing conflict.

www.ingramcontent.com/pod-product-compliance
Lightning Source LLC
Chambersburg PA
CBHW051204170526
45158CB00005B/1805